Delaney's Adventures – with Friends

Annette McCollough Myers & Delaney Ann Myers

This book is dedicated to all my friends and their parents, my mom and dad, my grandparents, my uncles, aunts and cousins, my elementary school teachers and the staff at ABC.

Library of Congress Control Number: 2020917245

FIRST EDITION (Hardcover) ISBN 978-0-9990514-5-0

Published by:
Giro di Mondo Publishing
Amelia Island, Florida
Contact: info@girodimondopublishing
www.girodimondopublishing.com

Edited by Emily Carmain, Noteworthy Editing
Cover and interior design by Roseanna White Designs
Background images and vector images from Shutterstock

PHOTO CREDITS: Donald and Dedria Myers, Annette Myers, Delaney Ann Myers
ABC Educational Childcare Center photo provided by Mrs. Laura Mackey, Owner and CEO
Printed in the United States of America

Giro di Mondo

HELLO!

My name is Delaney Ann Myers. Some people call me Laney. Others call me Lane Lane.

I was born October 14, 2010, in Savannah, Georgia, at Memorial Hospital. I'm now ten years old.

MEET OUR NEW
Baby Girl

Delaney Ann Myers 10/14/2010

My parents say I was just a bundle of joy!

My parents are Dedria Roberts Myers
and Donald Patrick Myers.

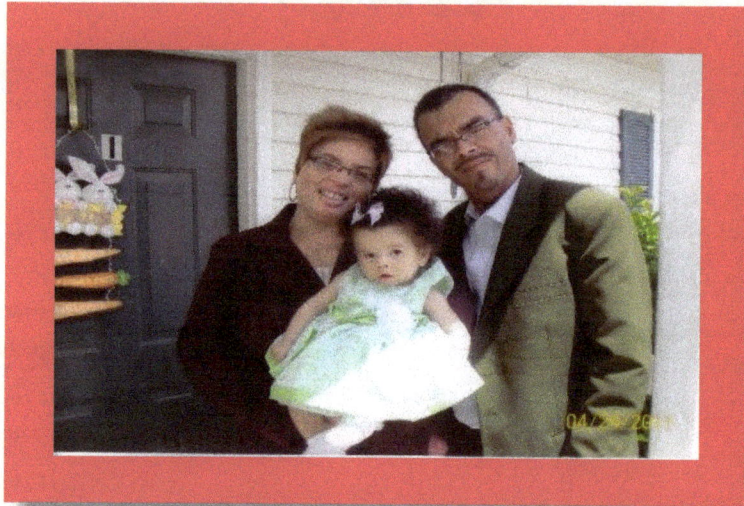

My middle name is Ann. Ann is part of my paternal
grandmother's first name. Her first name is Annette.

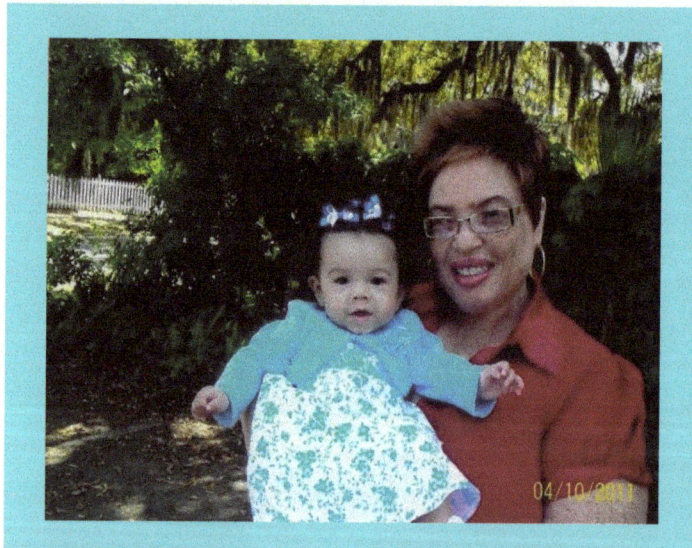

My mother manages a children's educational daycare center, called ABC Educational Childcare Center. I have been going to ABC with my mother since I was three months old.

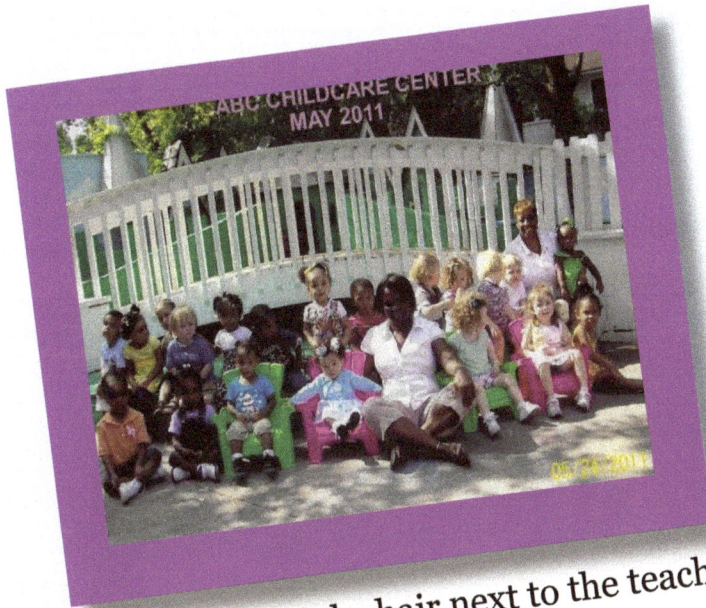

I'm in the hot pink chair next to the teacher.

Now, I'm in the fourth grade.

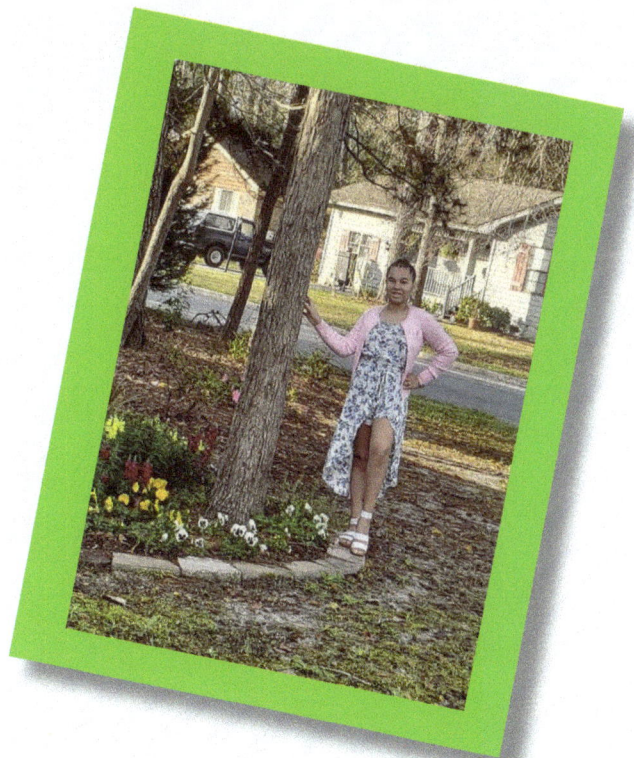

At the center, I have become friends and playmates with many other children. We have had lots of adventures together. My friends from daycare come from all backgrounds. Some of my friends are African American, some are Caucasian and some are Hispanic.

My best friend's name is Trinity. She is an eleven-year-old African American girl. Her mom, who used to be my babysitter, also works at the daycare.

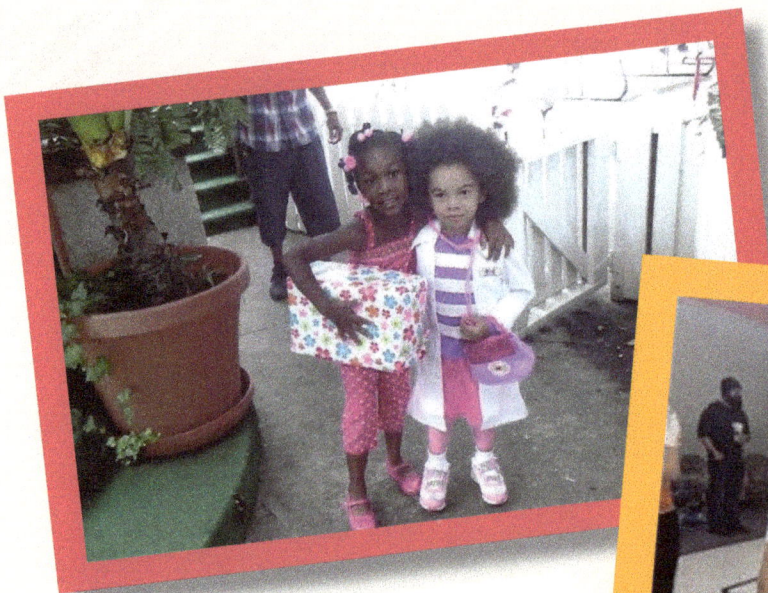

My friend Trinity at my
Doc McStuffins birthday party

Hanging out with Trinity
at the 'Y'

My Motto

Do you have a motto?

Do you have a Girl Scout or Boy Scout motto?

A motto is a short sentence or group of words you like or live by.

My motto is:

> " It is fun to have good friends. "

My school motto is: "Be proud of who you are, work hard to succeed and obey your parents."

5

ZODIAC SIGNS

Do you know anything about Zodiac signs or what sign you were born under? Well, I don't know much about Zodiac signs either, but this is how my grandmother, Annette, explains it.

The Zodiac is a path of space around Earth. It is the path that the Sun appears to take around Earth in a year. It is actually the Earth that moves around the Sun.

Twelve groups of stars - called constellations- lie in the traditional Zodiac of the Western world. Your Zodiac sign, or star sign, reflects the position of the Sun on the day you were born. Each sign is connected to different personality traits.

What are the Zodiac signs and dates, you might ask?

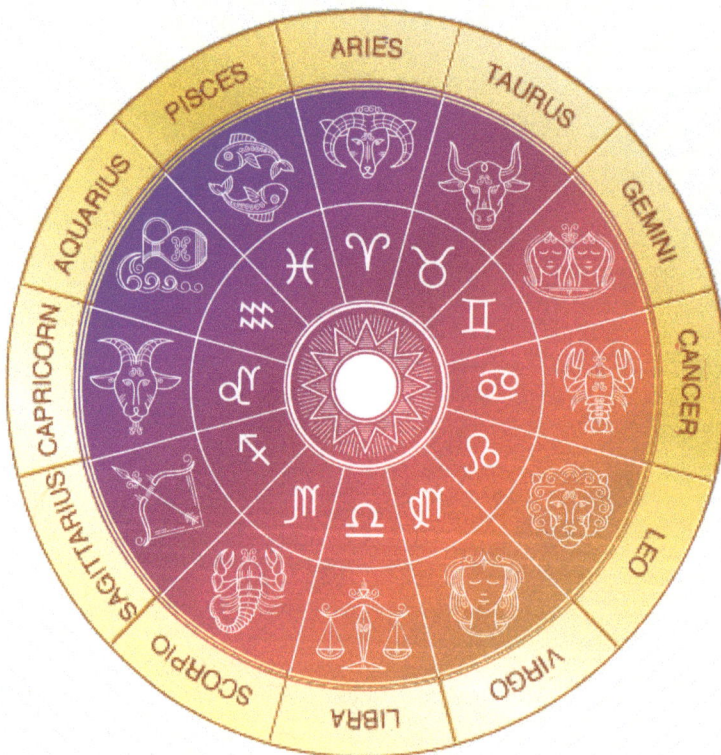

Signs of the Traditional Western Zodiac

To find your Zodiac sign, look for your birthday.

Capricorn	Dec. 22 - Jan. 19
Aquarius	Jan. 20 - Feb. 18
Pisces	Feb. 19 - Mar. 20
Aries	Mar. 21 - April 19
Taurus	April 20 - May 20
Gemini	May 21 - June 21
Cancer	June 22 - July 22
Leo	July 23 - Aug. 22
Virgo	Aug. 23 - Sept. 22
Libra	Sept. 23 - Oct. 23
Scorpio	Oct. 24 - Nov. 21
Sagittarius	Nov. 22 - Dec. 21

Because I was born on October 14, my Zodiac sign is Libra. Libras are described as serious, charming, graceful, and of good humor. Libras have a tendency to draw people to them. They are attractive and harmonious. They are sociable and get along with other people.

Do you know your Zodiac sign and what it means?

My friends are born at different times of the year. So their Zodiac sign is different from mine. All of us have different personality traits. Everyone is different, but the good news is that we all get along well together.

Birthday Adventures

Some of my best adventures have been as part of my birthday celebrations. Each year since I turned one, my parents have given me birthday parties with a theme. This year, 2020, will be my tenth birthday party.

My friends at daycare all come to my birthday parties, and I go to theirs.

Every year, my party has a theme and my friends come dressed according to the theme. We have so much fun! Here are the themes of my parties:

Year one	Dora and Friends
Year two	Peek-A-Boo: Guess Who's Two
Year three	Minnie Mouse
Year four	Doc McStuffins
Year five	My Little Pony: Friendship Is Magic
Year six	Cowboy Cowgirl Western Birthday
Year seven	Power Rangers
Year eight	Under the Sea
Year nine	Sparkly Unicorn
Year ten	We learn from Books

Some of my birthday parties have been at the Red Gate Farms Trail in Savannah, Georgia, some in Augusta, Georgia, and some have been at the ABC Center.

My ninth birthday was at our new home in Savannah.

My friends and I had a great time at my
Sparkly Unicorn party.

My Home

My new house

Savannah, Georgia,
where my family and I live.

This is my bedroom in my new house.

I also have many friends in my new bedroom.
They stay with me night and day.

Some of my bedroom friends are Unicorns,
Snoopy the Dog, Dumbo the Elephant, Dory the Fish,
Olaf the Snowman, Bow Bow the Dog, Lumme the Llama,
Kitty the Cat, Browndog the Dog, and Dora the Explorer.

Dora is my best bedtime friend.

Many of my bedroom friends were given to me
by my parents, grandparents, aunts, uncles, cousins,
and ABC friends.

Some of my best adventures are

Sports and Athletics

I am very active. It's healthy to be active.

I play basketball and soccer.

I like to ride my bicycle, walk the treadmill and skate on a skateboard.

I like most sports, but I LOVE SWIMMING.

What sports or activities do you like?

My 2019-20 Basketball Team and my trophy

For Entertainment

In my spare time, I like playing with my mommy's iPad.

There are lots of games and videos on the iPad.

There are also lots of games and videos on my tablet and my MacBook Pro.

I like watching Roblox, Clawee, Pastel Girl, Cartoon Network, Disney Now, Toca Life: World, Draw it, Trivia.io, Merge Dragons, Slimeatory, Disney+, Game of Songs and Gacha Life.

I like watching television, too.

My favorite shows are Wild 'N Out, Flintstones, SpongeBob SquarePants, Victorious, Arthur, Curious George, Wild Kratts, Phineas and Ferb, Adventure Time, Rugrats, The Magic School Bus, Henry Danger, The Loud House, The Thundermans, Just Roll with It, Game Shakers, Nicky, Ricky, Dicky & Dawn, and The Fairly OddParents.

What do you like to do for entertainment?

I have been very fortunate to have lots of adventures in other places.

Some of the places I have been are: Disney World, Six Flags Over Georgia, the Amelia Island Shrimp Festival and Kids Zone, UniverSoul Circus, Miami Seaquarium, Ellis Island National Museum of Immigration, the MLK Jr. Center in Atlanta, Georgia, the Jacksonville Zoo and the Statue of Liberty in New York.

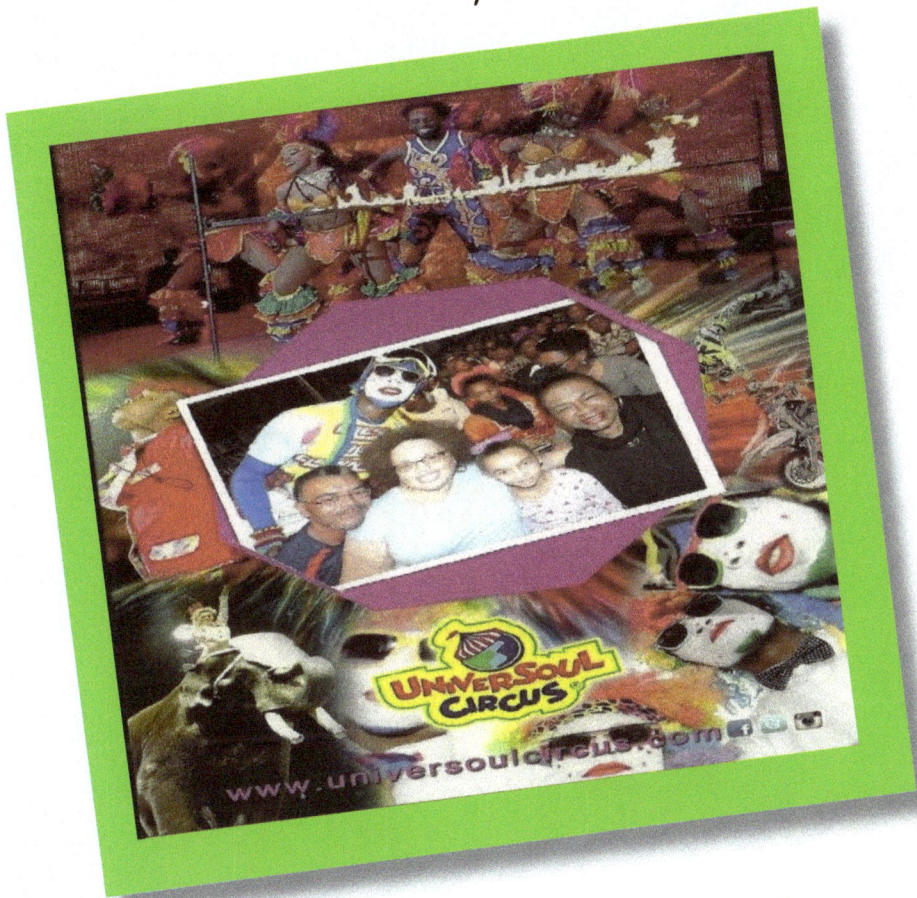

Fun with my family at the UniverSoul Circus, February 2017

Adventures at School

School is a place where my friends and I experience lots of adventures.

When I turned four years old, I started going to a Montessori school from pre-k to second grade. Now I go to Jacob G. Smith Elementary School, but I still go to ABC after school and stay there until my mom gets off from work. The ABC bus picks me up.

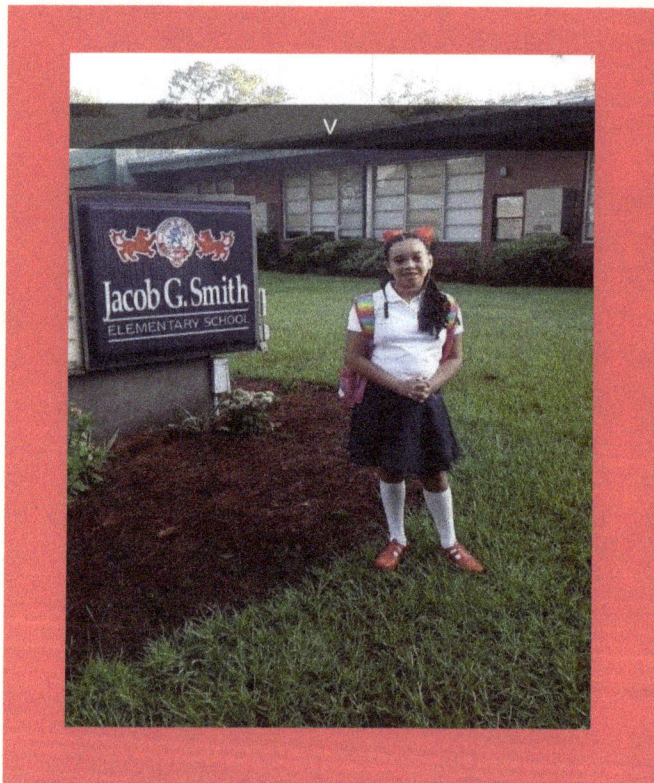

Third Grade - 2019-20

Subjects I enjoy at school are Math, Chorus, Physical Education, Latin, Language Arts, Writing and Art.

I am on the Principal's Honor Roll List. But sometimes I need help with some of my subjects, so I talk to my mom about it and she gets me a tutor in certain subjects because I always want to get good grades.

If you want to be a successful student, you have to study hard, and do your school homework on time.

Do you sometimes need extra help with schoolwork? My grandmother says, "It's always okay to ask for help."

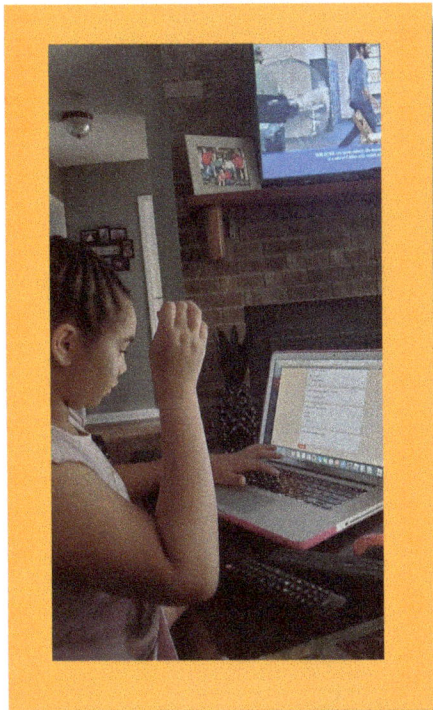

When I graduate from high school, I plan to go to college and get a college degree. I want to become a veterinarian (a vet doctor) and a business owner.

I want to become a vet doctor because I like animals and maybe I can own a vet clinic.

A Cell Phone

When I turned nine years old, my parents allowed me to have a cell phone.

I am so happy to have a cell phone. I enjoy calling and talking to my friends and my grandparents when I am out of school or on the weekends.

My Grandparents

I am very fortunate to have grandparents.
I visit my grandparents during the holidays and during the summer months. My maternal grandmother's name is Bertha. My paternal grandmother's name is Annette.

Bertha Roberts
My mother's mom

Annette Myers
My dad's mom

Both my mommy's father and my daddy's father are deceased. They were my granddads.

My New Puppy, Duke

I have always wanted a dog. In March 2020, I got a Yorkshire Terrier named Duke. He is the latest addition to my family. Duke is five months old. Since I am the only child in my family, I am elated to have Duke.

We have lots of fun exploring together. One of the best adventures I've tackled since getting Duke is learning how to take good care of him.

Delaney's Photo Gallery

Do you have a photo album of people you love and good times you've enjoyed?

Mom and Dad — 2000

Trying out some fashion sunshades at nineteen months old

Christmas 2012 — Two years old

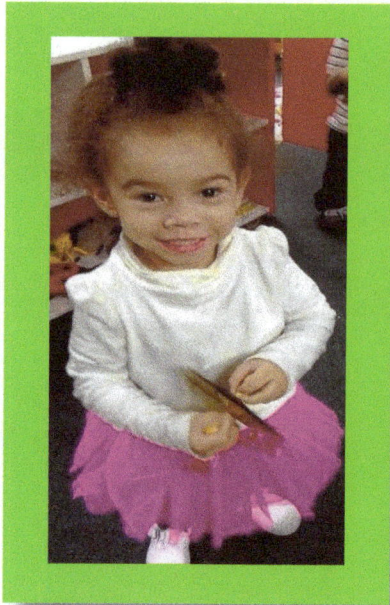
At Guess Who's Two
birthday party – 2012

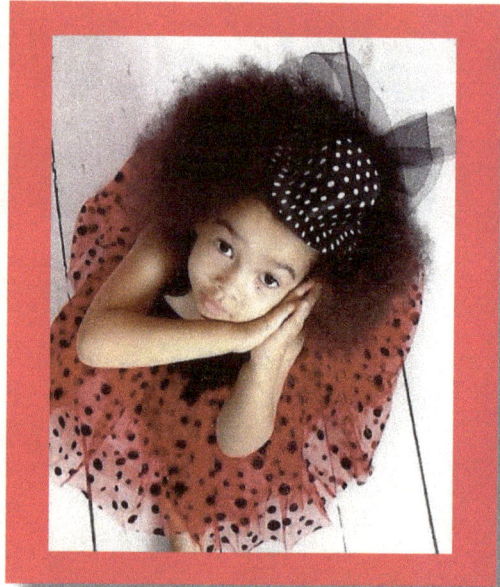
Three years old – 2013

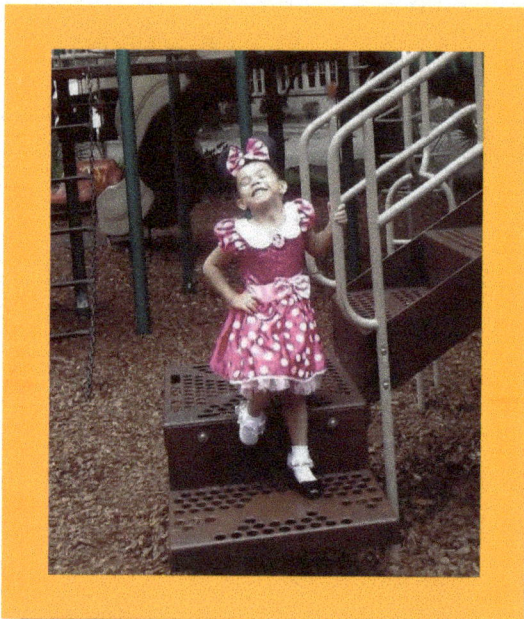
Delaney Mouse four years
old – 2014

My Little Pony birthday party
October 2015 — Five years old

Cowboy Cowgirl birthday party
October 23, 2016, at Red Gate Farms Trail

Mom and me

Cowgirl Delaney

Dad on horseback

Grandmom Annette

Beginning first grade

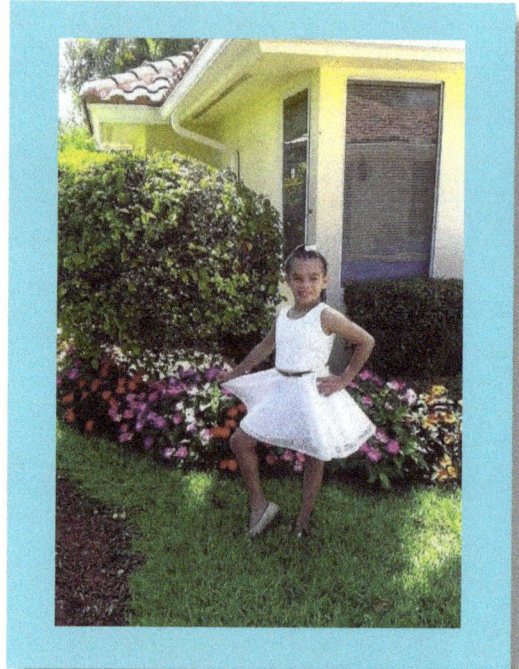
Seven years old –
April 2017

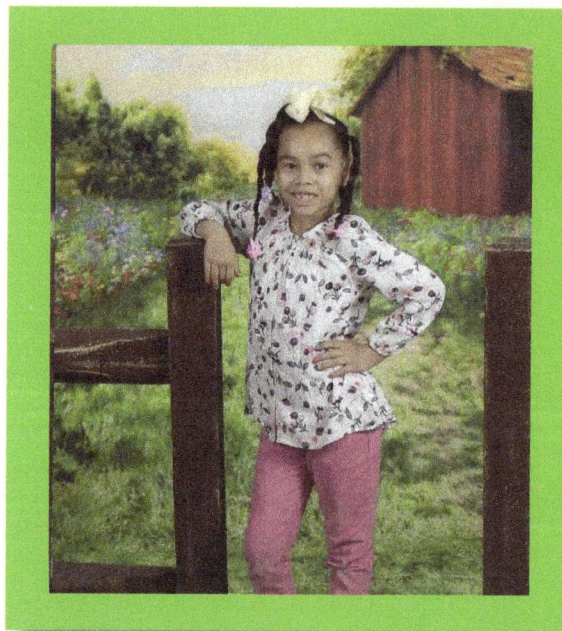
At Red Gate Farms Trail – 2017

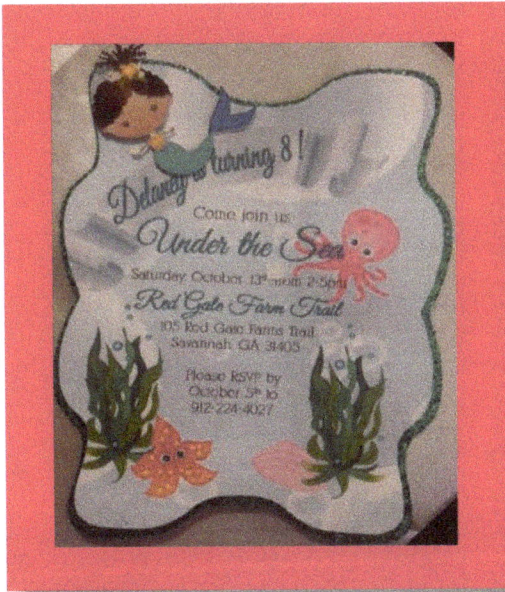

My mother usually sends out a very special invitation for my birthday. Here's my eight-year-old birthday party invitation.

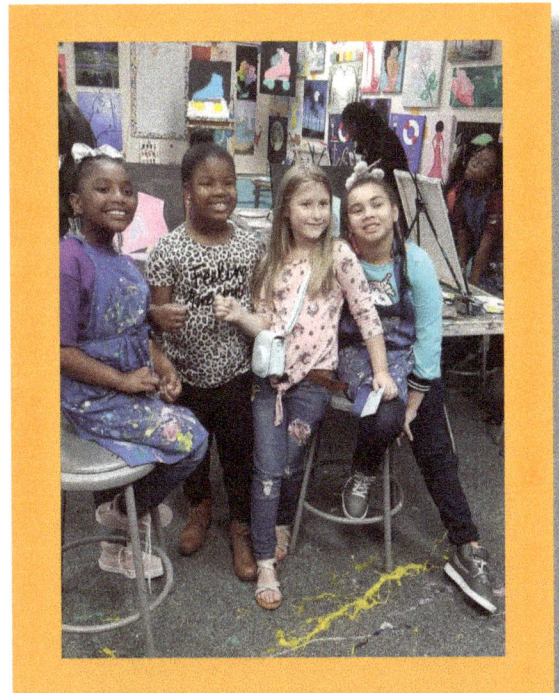

With some ABC and school friends — 2020

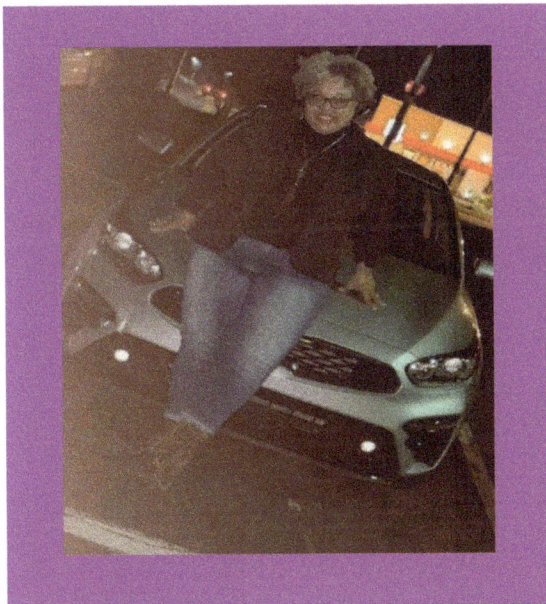

Aunt Bertina — my mom's sister

Aunt Barbara — Grandmom Annette's sister

Grandmom Annette and
me — nine years old

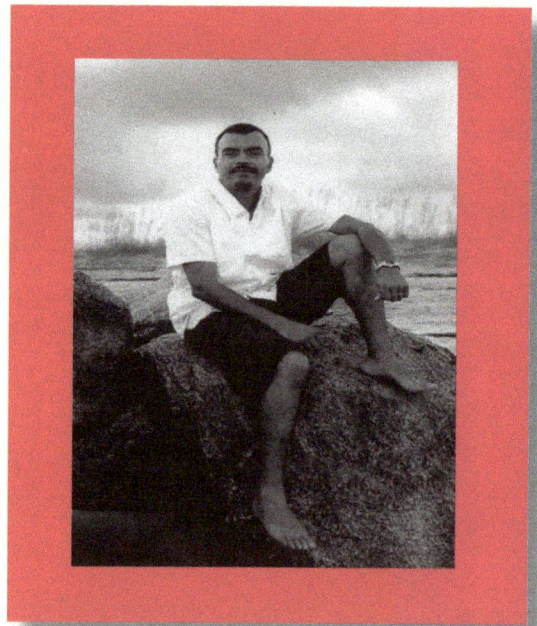

Dad — awaiting my arrival
in the fall of 2010

My mom's dad —
Timothy Roberts, my
granddad, who passed away
on January 10, 2020.

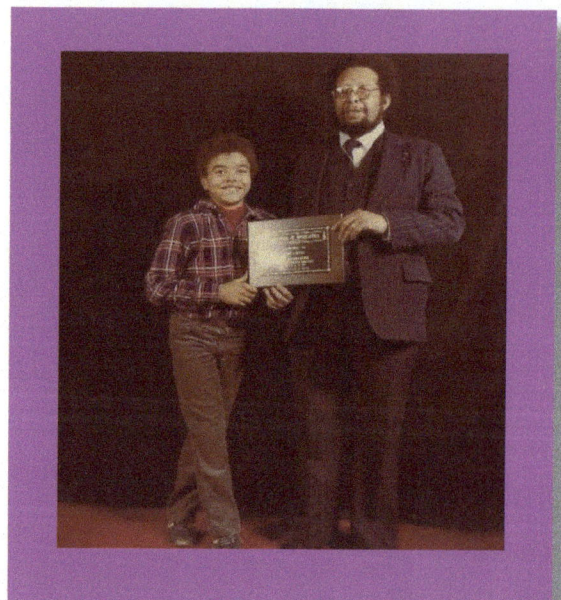

My dad Don and his dad in 1981
— Elmo Myers, my granddad,
who passed away in April 1987.

Questions to help you create your own Adventures

1. When were you born?

2. In what city and state where you born?

3. What is your Zodiac sign?

4. How many Zodiac signs are there?

5. What is the name of your best friend?

6. If you could have a birthday party theme, what would you choose?

7. What do you want to do after you finish school?

8. Delaney has a pet. Do you have a pet? What type and what is its name?

9. What are the names of your maternal grandmother and your maternal grandfather?

10. Do you know the names of your paternal grandmother and grandfather?

11. Delaney has a motto. Do you remember what it is?

12. Do you have a motto?

13. If not, can you experiment with developing one?

14. Name your best adventure so far in your life?

15. What adventures are you still waiting to have?

Vocabulary Words

ADVENTURE - an unusual and exciting, sometimes hazardous, experience or activity

CONSTELLATION - a group of stars forming a recognizable pattern that is traditionally named after its apparent form or identified with a mythological figure

DECEASED - passed away

ELATED - happy, excited

ENTERTAINMENT - Fun things or activities we enjoy that make us happy

EXPERIMENT - to try something

FORTUNATE - blessed; lucky

MATERNAL - having to do with your mother

MOTTO - words or phrase to live by

PATERNAL - having to do with your father

PLAN - a detailed scheme for accomplishing something

TACKLED - made a determined effort to deal with a difficult task or problem

TUTOR - a person with experience to help you with a subject or school lessons

USUALLY - most often

About the Authors

Annette McCollough Myers

Annette Myers is a National Indie Excellence Award winning author. She is a Fernandina Beach, Florida, Nassau County native, community activist, and a retired Nassau County educator and guidance counselor. She has taught in the public school system of Florida on various levels, including Florida State College at Jacksonville. Since retirement, she has published three nonfiction books about historic American Beach, which lies on the south end of Amelia Island in Fernandina Beach, Florida. Her latest nonfiction book about her high school alma mater, *PECK High School — Golden Years Remembered*, was published in 2017.

Annette is well traveled in and out of the United States. She lives in American Beach, in northeast Florida, where she is a long-time property owner and the owner of her home, Martha's Hideaway, which was listed on the National Register of Historic Places October 12, 2001.

Annette earned her Bachelor of Science degree from Florida A&M University in Tallahassee, Florida, her Master of Science degree from Indiana State University, Terre Haute, Indiana, and her Educational Specialist degree from Nova University in Fort Lauderdale, Florida.

She is the proud grandmother of Delaney Ann Myers and loving mother of son Donald Myers (wife Dedria) and foster daughter Alria Wilson Mundy.

Delaney Ann Myers

Delaney, in 2020, is a fourth grade student at Jacob G. Smith Elementary School where she is an honor student who loves to read.

She lives in Savannah, Georgia, with her parents. She has enjoyed visiting quite a few places and attractions, such as Disney World, Six Flags Over Georgia, the Amelia Island Shrimp Festival and Kids Zone, UniverSoul Circus, Miami Seaquarium, Ellis Island National Museum of Immigration, the MLK Jr. Center in Atlanta, Georgia, the Jacksonville Zoo and the Statue of Liberty in New York.

Delaney is proud to be the co-author of this book along with her paternal grandmother Annette.

www.ingramcontent.com/pod-product-compliance
Lightning Source LLC
Chambersburg PA
CBHW040257100426
42811CB00011B/1289